Deliverance Is Available To You

Motivation to Move Forward

Deliverance Is Available To You

Motivation to Move Forward

Joy L. Wilkerson

Foreword by Reverends Kenneth S. and Marilynn S. Robinson

BASAR
PUBLISHING

ISBN: 978-1-942013-33-4

Cover design by Darlene Newman
Edited by Lou Paris and Nikkele Shelton
Author Photo by JustInVision Photography

Printed in the United States of America by Basar Publishing.

DEDICATION

I give God all the glory for the people that He has placed in my life who have graced my growth, spirit, soul and body. For this I give God praise!

TABLE OF CONTENTS

FOREWORD

We are most appreciative of Rev. Joy Wilkerson's marvelous and surprisingly honest account of her own journey, and of the seasons and the soils through which she has travelled. It is rare today - especially in faith circles - that a minister would disclose so much so willingly, for the altruistic benefit of her readers, without having a more narcissistic motive.

As we read her book, we see on display the "E" in D.A.N.C.E., which - as Joy identifies it - represents "evidence." She is herself, the evidence. Herein, she replays, relays, and portrays the evidence - the transparent and authentic witness - of her own, personal life story. What she has done is, indeed, akin to the legacy that we have in Jesus; who thought it not robbery to make Himself very human, to be transparently on display for all the world to see. In the kerygma of His life, we saw not only the glory, but also the pathos of His story; not only the majesty of the Spring times and Summers of His ministry, but also the dark, dreary and depressing days of His Falls and Winters. The testimony of Joy's faith walk is the "evidence of things hoped for" - her aspiration and total confidence that deliverance is available.

Joy takes us artfully through the pilgrimage of illness, denial, awareness, outreach and wholeness; identifying elements that contribute to both resistance to and facilitation of healing and recovery. She helps the reader understand how to achieve a marvelous balance between the spiritual and the clinical; and how to synthesize, integrate and reconcile both the counsel of pastors and the therapeutics of physicians. Her own walk reminds us that while deliverance is, indeed, available - as is water to a thirsty horse at the river, healing to a person who is undeniably ill, and The Word to one who needs to be saved - we must recognize, reach, and receive that deliverance which God has for us all.

We believe that The Spirit of The Lord is with Joy; and, therefore, that deliverance is available to her and to the readers of this work. May Joy always DANCE!

Rev. Kenneth S. Robinson, M.D., M.Div.
Rev. Marilynn S. Robinson, M.P.H.
Pastors, St. Andrew A.M.E. Church
Memphis, TN

PREFACE

There has been a book inside of me waiting to come out for a long time. However, I was not able to begin writing until I shared my testimony. The first two chapters, Struggling in the Thorns and Delivered to Good Ground, are my testimony. It was not until I shared my testimony with a group outside of my church family that the pen began to flow across the page. After the verbal release of my testimony with my Formation for Ministry Covenant Group in seminary, I was able to write the story that God was calling me to share so his people can be delivered and set free. At one of our *Dance the Word* Liturgical Dance Conferences, I prophesied over myself through dance that *the Lord is calling me to write the vision and make it plain to help the mentally ill deal with the battlefield of their mind so that they can be set free, set free, set free!*

The mentally ill are not just the people walking down the street talking to themselves. They are not just the homeless schizophrenics who refuse to stay on their medication. We all, from time to time, experience bouts of depression or severe mood swings because of things going on in our lives. Most of us are able to cope successfully, or so it appears, without seeking professional counseling or having to take medication. But so many more, more than you know, are suffering in silence. The pressures of living this thing called life are weighing us down. We are operating functionally depressed but, truth be told, if we went to a doctor we might be diagnosed clinically depressed. However, instead of seeking help we keep trudging along until it is almost too late. We seriously think about suicide—harming ourselves and/or others—but we get pulled back just in the nick of time.

Unfortunately, some are successful in their suicide or murder/suicide attempts, leaving the people behind asking why. Sometimes those left behind will acknowledge signs that they ignored. "I always thought something was wrong." But more often than not, "I thought they had it together. They seemed happy." But little do you know about the battle raging in their minds. Their expectation for their lives, whether realistic or seemingly realistic, was not being met, and the harder they tried to get it right the more quickly things were falling apart.

God says, "I'll fight your battle" – mind, body and soul. The battle is already won if we would think on these things: "Whatever is true, whatever is noble, whatever is right, whatever is pure, whatever is lovely, whatever is admirable—if anything is excellent or praiseworthy—think about such things" (Philippians 4:8 NIV). Ephesians 4:23 in the Amplified Bible says, "And be constantly renewed in the spirit of your mind [having a fresh mental and spiritual attitude]."

As I began the journey to author my first book, I realized that God was calling me to help his sons and daughters deal with the battles in their lives so they can be delivered and set free—so that they can have renewed minds. The struggles that we face and the situations that we deal with on a daily basis as we walk out this thing called life weigh heavily on our minds. There is a battle going on in our minds and it may make us feel like we are going crazy or suffering from mental illness. But understand that the situations and struggles that we are facing are temporary, and we cannot take permanent actions to resolve temporary problems. Yes, mental illness is real, but just because you are going through a season of depression as the result of a situation in your life does not mean you suffer from a chronic mental illness. There is a difference between situational depression and chronic depression. A chronic condition is always present or recurring. A situation relates to our current circumstances.

Situations and circumstances change just like seasons of the year. Just as there are winter, spring, summer and fall, there are seasons of our lives. Every season is not going to be warm and sunny. As we go through our falls and winters we are going to experience hurt and pain, and we are going to experience seasons of grief due to the loss of a loved one. We might experience grief over the loss of a child. We may experience seasons of depression over a job loss or being unable to find a job after graduating from college. We could experience a season of depression over the loss of a home. It's possible that we may even experience disappointment over receiving an unwanted medical diagnosis. The list goes on. We are going to experience fall and winter, but I am here to let you know that spring and summer are coming. Better is coming and you can overcome! Walk into your season; deliverance is available to you.

INTRODUCTION

My fall and winter were experienced in the "thorns", the trying times, as will be described in Chapter One. However, as my Pastor did a Bible Study series on W.W.J.D. (What Would Jesus Do?) and taught on Mark 4, the parable of the sower, my desire to be transformed from the seed that fell among the thorns to the seed that fell on good ground began. Chapter Two tells how I was delivered to good ground. Deliverance did not happen overnight and it did not happen miraculously. I had to take responsibility for my life with God as my guide. In order to begin the deliverance process, one must recognize that they have something from which they need to be delivered. Often we are in bondage to things or people and do not realize it. We have been going along with the status quo for so long that we think everything is okay, but once we recognize the bondage, once we recognize the chains and we make a decision to be set free, we must have a plan of action. There has to be intentionality in getting your life back.

My deliverance came through dance—liturgical dance. Liturgical comes from the root word liturgy. Liturgy is defined as a "Eucharistic" rite. Eucharist is what the early church referred to when they spoke of the consecrated bread partaken during the sacrament of Holy Communion. A rite is defined as that which is ceremonial in nature done specifically as an act of dedication and worship to God. Now everyone is not going to get their breakthrough as they participate in or witness liturgical dance. Rather, deliverance must come by expressing one's faith as an act of dedication and worship to God. Spiritual communion with God is necessary in order to be released and set free.

Each one's process is different, but I explain my process by breaking down D.A.N.C.E. The "D" represents dedicated. It means being dedicated, faithful, loyal and committed to Christ. The "A" represents avid. Another word for avid is passionate. In order to experience release from whatever is keeping you bound—mentally, physically or spiritually—one needs to have something he or she is passionate about. One must be avid about an activity, a cause, a practice, or a hobby, and have something to focus on in order to press forward and not be bogged down in one's current condition. Remember, it is just a season. The "N" represents nourished by spiritual disciplines. Spiritual practices like reading, meditating on the word, fasting, and praying are vital to your breakthrough. The "C" represents care for the soul through a confidant or counselor. God is always there, but God works through humans. Find a person who you can trust and/or seek professional counseling. And lastly, the "E" represents evident. You must be evident. What I mean by this, is you must be transparent and authentic. No, you cannot tell everybody everything, but God will guide you and direct on when and what to share and with whom. Your testimony—your truth—will set someone free.

In order to walk into your new season, you must be intentional. You will not always feel like going to church, preaching the Word, going to Bible Study, etc., but spiritual practices are foundational. When you are going through your bitter seasons, it is not the time to withdraw. Sometimes I did not feel like dancing. Sometimes I was going through the motions of living, but I kept going.

In June 2005, I attended a local Sisterhood Showcase and Rev. Claudette Copeland preached a word, **Jesus Can Straighten You Out** (Luke 10:11-13). One point that she illustrated was that you must keep showing up. No matter how long it has been, 18 days or 18 years, you have got to "stick and stay". She said that delay will dim the hope of your deliverance. It makes cowards of us. But if you are going to be a story of remembrance, you have got to keep showing up until you get the manifestation. I have experienced many ups and downs, the most significant occurring between January 2001 and January 2006. Yet, the Lord is working a work in me and has placed me exactly where He wants me to be to receive the manifestation.

Over the course of this book I will elaborate on D.A.N.C.E. Rev. Sarita M. Wilson, author of Dance the Word, says that "dance tells a story, your story and your journey. It is a private inner movement that, when shared, testifies and tells the story of your life. Dance is you...unveiled. It revives. It renews. Dance is freeing. We release all of our past, our guilt and shame, our heartbreaks and disappointments into the abyss of a whirl, a leap or a contraction" (7-8). I do D.A.N.C.E., and I pray that as you read this book these steps will renew your spirit and give you strength to overcome whatever season you are walking through. Trust and believe that better is coming...the spring flowers will bloom again and the summer suns will shine. Walk into your season. Deliverance is available to you.

STRUGGLING IN THE THORNS

Why do we care what the world thinks? Why are we seeking to keep up with the Joneses? Each of us is given gifts according to the grace that is given to us, and the Word says to use them. However, we always want what someone else has—their gifts, their possessions, their spouses, their jobs, their lives. We live in a materialistic world, and we care more about what others think than what God wants. Many of us are not content to produce good fruit with what God has given us. Mark 4: 1-20 describes the parable of the sower. There was seed that fell by the wayside. There was seed that fell on stony ground, seed that fell among the thorns and there was also seed that fell on good ground.

I want to spend some time on the thorny ground. See, *the seed that fell among the thorns, the thorns grew up and choked it and it yielded no crop. The sower was sowing the Word. Now these are the ones sown among thorns. They are the ones who hear the Word and the cares of the world, the deceitfulness of riches and the desires for other things entering in choke the Word and it becomes unfruitful.* How did I come to be among the thorns?

When I was young and carefree, growing up in a rural area, I did not think much about the fact that my family did not have indoor plumbing. My brother and I were best friends. In the summers we rode our bikes and played outdoors until the sun went down. We talked, watched television, and listened to music. It was not until I became a teenager that I really began to notice that we did not have what others had, and I began to care what the world thought. I began to care that I did not have designer jeans and name brand shoes. I began to hurt when a girl, not normally on our bus route, was going home with one of her friends and laughed uncontrollably when the bus stopped in front of our house and we got off.

I think it must have been then that I decided I was going to get out. I gave up the notion of being popular in high school and conceded to being a nerd because I was going to get out of my hometown. The only way I knew to escape was education so I had to focus on the books to qualify for a scholarship. I could not afford to get pregnant. I'm not saying you cannot have a fulfilling life after a teenage pregnancy, but there were no success stories in my hometown at the time. I was determined to get out and there could be no obstacles in my way.

When I graduated from high school, I was going to college and get a good job. When I graduated I was going to have what I wanted when I wanted. I was definitely a seed planted amongst the thorns. Unfortunately, I discovered in college that I did not have to wait until I graduated and got a job to have what I wanted. Credit became my best friend.

From my freshman year to my senior year, my use of credit was manageable (or so I thought). I earned enough from campus jobs to make my minimum payments. But after college it only got worse. By the time I graduated, I was so deep in debt that almost all of my paychecks went to paying bills. Because I had no cash, I used credit cards to live so the debt never decreased. After working three years, I decided to go back to school full-time to get an MBA. The debt did not disappear; it only increased.

When I graduated with my MBA, my salary was more than double what I previously earned, but I did not use this as an opportunity to free myself from debt. I just increased my standard of living. I went from silver to gold with my credit and kept on doing what I had been doing. I was single with no dependents but I was living paycheck to paycheck. As long as I could pay the bills when they came, I was not bothered. In 1998, despite my debt-to-equity ratio, I decided to buy a house. The Lord was nowhere in my financial decision. I even stopped tithing leading up to the purchase so that I would have money for the down payment. I was buying things—doings things in an attempt to make myself happy—but all the while I was mired in depression. I was about to turn 30 and still single with no children. ALL of my friends were marrying, buying houses, and starting families. The only thing that I could do by myself was buy a house, so I did.

On closing day there was no joy, and on moving day in October I was not excited. On my thirtieth birthday in November 1998 I was not happy. I continued to "fake the funk", or pretend everything was okay, until I could take it no more. In January 2001 my position was eliminated. While I secured a new job with a premier company in Memphis, I was going to take a $19,000 pay cut. Living from paycheck to paycheck and taking a $19,000-a-year pay cut was a little more than I could bear. I wanted to believe that God would make everything right, but my logic—my analytical mind—just could not see past the numbers and past all of my bills. Ultimately I got to the edge of the cliff and fell off.

We all have experiences that bring us to the edge. Some get close enough to look over the edge and are ready to surrender before they fall off. Others, like me, kept testing the edge so that when it arrived they did not realize it was there and toppled over, seemingly unexpected. However, it happened over a period of time. They knew it was there; they were just in denial. Regardless of how you got to the edge or why you fell off—job or lack thereof, career (secular or ministry) not moving the way you want, your health, your marriage, your children, the loss of a loved one, your addiction (alcohol, drugs, sexing, eating, etc.)—I am here to share with you that you can overcome. You can become seed-producing in good ground and bear good fruit.

God is the God of our breakthrough. Over the next chapters I will share what happened when I fell off the edge. More importantly I will share how I got back up and kept moving forward. The Lord knew what was going to happen before I did, and even before I got to that point God had given me the dance. The Lord had given me an "in spite of yet praise!" We, the Liturgical Dance ministry, ministered to Kurt Carr's Every Mountain and I truly gave the Father praise. *For every mountain you've brought me over. For every trial you've seen me through. For every blessing, Hallelujah! For this I give you praise.* My praise has been my support. My praise has been the anchor that has carried me through. For this I give God praise. Whatever you are going through, give God the praise. The test and trials will only make you stronger. Believe God for a good crop.

DELIVERED TO GOOD GROUND

But the other seed fell on good ground and yielded a crop that sprang up, increased and produced some thirty, some sixty, and some a hundred. I survived the fall. When I awoke, I found myself in the psychiatric ward of Saint Francis Hospital. The weight of years of living beyond my means had become too much. When my job was eliminated and I had to take a significant pay cut, it was more than I could bear at the time. Because I was struggling in the thorns trying – wanting so desperately to be on good ground. But, I kept vacillating between depending on myself and depending on God. God is El Shaddai, the all-sufficient one. I am not sure that I knew that at the time and if I knew, I surely did not fully believe.

Well after my experience from early 2001 until early 2006, I know without a shadow of a doubt that the great "I AM THAT I AM" IS, ALWAYS and SHALL BE. Jehovah Jireh provided for me. My stay in the hospital was brief, maybe ten days, but life was dramatically changed after that. That was the beginning of a long period of brokenness. I went from a severe pay cut to being unemployed. I thought the initial hit of being unemployed and mentally unstable was the worst but this was followed by a long period of depression that did not end until March 2006. Before I get to March 2006, I will share briefly what happened in between.

At the time, I felt that I had lost everything, but I was looking with worldly vision. I lost my new job that I never even got to start, I had to move out of my house, could no longer pay my bills, and lost my professional MBA status. Unemployed from the end of January until shortly after 9/11, I lived off of my 401(k) and minimal savings. I did some volunteer work through my church, but for the most part I was inactive. I was depressed, sitting at home doing nothing but eating and watching TV, and thinking "Why me? When will this be over?" I had a few job interviews here and there, but emotionally I was not ready to return to work. I was just trying to force my life back to normal. I gained a significant amount of weight over a short period of time. I was broken.

I was under-employed from September 2001 through mid-January 2006. My first job was an hourly one making slightly more than minimum wage. Me, a college educated woman, with an undergraduate degree in accounting and an MBA from The University of Michigan, was punching a clock. Say it isn't so! I was both depressed and broken. God was taking care of me, but not in the way I wanted to be. So in November 2002, I took a salaried position just so I could say I was working a professional job. I had an office but I was not happy. God did not tell me to take that job, and day by day I became more miserable. One thing I learned is that money and status are not important if you do not have peace of mind and rest in the comfort of the Father.

Ultimately I was at the point of dreading going to work, and many days I did not make it to work. Eventually I gave notice lest I get fired. Because I quit I was not able to draw unemployment. I returned to temporary agencies and ended up with a long-term temporary assignment by day beginning in March 2004, and shortly thereafter I began working part-time overnight at FedEx Hub operations to have medical benefits. Now that is a humbling experience for a highly educated, "MBA-toting" individual! This lasted for almost two years. Many days and nights during this time I asked the Lord, "Why?" As much as I asked the Lord that question when I became hospitalized, I asked even more, "Why does this continue? Haven't I endured enough? Whenever it seems that things are getting better, something else happens. When will it end? I am tired...I'm just sick and tired of being sick and tired." But I have often heard the phrase, "You will understand it better by and by." While I don't understand everything, I do understand "better."

In the midst of this I continued to go to church and participate in ministry. I remember one day I felt like if God didn't move I would lose my mind. I could not understand how I could be a born-again believer and go through something like this. I wondered sometimes if I were under a curse, and at times I even had the strong delusion that maybe I was suffering for the anointing. The scriptures say to reign with him you must suffer with him. Aha! I thought I had the answer. But then I read the scripture, with all they getting get an understanding, and that was when I realized it was not about the anointing, suffering to reign, or even a curse. I was suffering due to my ignorance and lack of temperance. I was suffering because I was trying to escape a past that I now know was by design in order to help me identify with the audience God really wants me to reach. You see, there are people who still use an outhouse today and they need to know that they can get OUT THE HOUSE and break the cycle of poverty. But not with credit cards and not with fancy clothes and shoes. The cycle is broken when we humble ourselves and learn not to despise small beginnings! The cycle is broken when we trust God as our source.

When I took the step to surrender and trust God, deliverance came. The Women's Season theme that year was "Valued and Victorious" based on Psalm 18:35 NIV: "You make your saving help my shield, and your right hand sustains me; your help has made me great". On Sisterhood Sunday, January 2006, we (Ministry in Motion Liturgical Dance Ministry) ministered to Vicki Yohe's "Deliverance is Available to You." Little did I know that was my deliverance song. At our prayer vigil in March I came forward in surrender and asked for prayer – prayer for emotional healing and release from a relationship that did not honor God. When I surrendered all to God, the floodgates were opened and I really felt like dancing. I was delivered as the cleansing tears rolled down my cheeks and I felt accepted again by Christ. I was nourished by the Words of the model prayer in Matthew 6.

The following Saturday was the annual Women's Retreat and at the end of the morning meditation service, the speaker said the Lord had been speaking to her and that she had come to the retreat for a particular person. She had actually showed up a week early. While we were at the prayer vigil at our church...she was at the conference center. As she continued to talk, she began playing "Deliverance is Available to You". I knew the person that she came for was me and I ran forward crying, "It's me!" She presented me with a Woman of Destiny 2006 Trophy...Valued and Victorious! On that Sunday at Women's Day service we ministered "Set Me Free!" by Myron Butler and Levi. I had a solo part based on the lyrics *I gave the Lord (yea) The Lord my life (yea). And in exchange, he gave me brand new life, I haven't been the same.* Yes, for a long time I was broken, but once I surrendered the potter molded me and shaped me and put me back together again. Since then I have not been the same. What does not kill you makes you stronger. Because of what I have been through, I know the Lord will carry me. He does sustain with his right hand!

From Sisterhood Sunday, January 29, 2006, I remember both the sermon and the song. Our Co-Pastor brought forth a word based on Exodus 2:1-8, 15:19-21, called, *I Hope You Dance*, "When the Red Sea is before you and Pharaoh's army is behind you, it's time to celebrate! When you have the choice to sit it out or dance, I hope you dance!" I choose to dance because **Deliverance Is Available** to me and I have received it. I have been delivered to good ground and you too can be delivered. The first two chapters of this work have been my testimony. As you go through your tests and overcome your trials, you too will have a testimony. If you need to have your spirit renewed. If you are looking to press your way to a breakthrough, then continue to read. You can overcome; deliverance is available to you.

DEDICATED TO CHRIST

As a child in North Carolina I grew up going to church. I was the child of a preacher's kid. My father was a deacon and he went to church regularly out of duty and obligation. This is not to say that he did not love the Lord for himself. However, as children we often do what our parents expect and continue as adults because that is what we have always done. My Dad wanted to make his father, Rev. J.E. Wilkerson, proud, and he took my brother and me to church with him every Sunday. I can still remember my father holding the offering plates with the other deacons. I was not that much into church, but I knew who Jesus was. I was baptized at an early age because it was expected.

Despite my early baptism, I did not have a personal relationship with the Lord. The Word says to train up a child in the way that they should go and, when they are old they will not depart from it. When I went to college, I established friendships with Christian people and went to church on a fairly regular basis at churches near campus. I knew that going to church was the "right" thing to do. It was not because Psalm 133: 1-3 says that it is good and pleasant for brethren to dwell together in unity, but because I was brought up going to church.

I was not involved in ministry and therefore was not spreading the gospel of Jesus Christ. It was not until my adult life, in my late twenties, that I really began to seek a relationship with Christ. Whereas in the past I only went to church on Sundays, I began to attend Bible Study. I was seeking to learn more about God through His Word. However, I was not consistent—I was straddling the fence between developing my relationship with God and maintaining my relationship with the world. It was a struggle for me to totally trust God as I was enamored by the material trappings of life—travel, clothes and entertainment. It was not until I came to a place of surrender that I began to develop my relationship with the Lord. It was not until I surrendered all to Christ that my deliverance came. It was not until I chose to live a dedicated life for Christ that things began to change. The first step is surrender. How do you get to a place of surrender?

A worship leader once asked the congregation, "How bad do you want it?" During my "going through" season I felt like the woman in Mark 5 with the issue of blood for twelve long years. How bad did she want to be healed? How bad did she want to be made whole? She had suffered a great deal under the care of many doctors and had spent all she had. When she heard about Jesus, she pressed her way, came up behind him in the crowd, and touched his cloak. She thought, "If I can just touch his clothes, I will be healed" (Mark 5:28).

I had to ask myself, "How bad do I want to be made whole?" How bad did I want to be set free from the ties that bind? How bad did I want to be lifted out of the slimy pit, the mud and mire, and have my feet set on a rock with a firm place to stand? (Psalm 40:2). I knew that if I touched the hem of his garment I would be made whole. I knew my deliverance would come. At our annual Sisters prayer vigil I pressed my way forward in surrender and asked for prayer—prayer for emotional healing and release from a wrong relationship. When I surrendered all to God the floodgates were opened, and I really felt like dancing. I was delivered as the cleansing tears rolled down my cheeks and I felt accepted again by Christ. I had returned to the first love that I knew—with the Father.

When you have been struggling with an issue for a very long time, you have possibly given up on God. To get back to that first love, you have to remember how God has kept you and trust God as your source for joy. Have you ever gone through a time in your life when you thought something would make you happy, and then when you got it, that thing did not make you happy at all? Maybe you were thrilled for a little while, but you soon realized it would not bring deep, lasting happiness to your life. Lots of people do that. They think they will be happy if they get a raise, or a new house, or a new car, or something else that money can buy. They are focused on what they can get, not what they can give. These pursuits never lead to happiness!

The Word says in Lamentations 3:24-25, "The Lord is my portion, saith my soul; therefore will I hope in him. The Lord is good unto them that wait for him, to the soul that seeketh him." The Lord is my portion. Everything that I need to bring me joy comes from the Lord. Happiness is a temporary state but joy unspeakable is always. All the situations and circumstances that I go through may not be joyful, but when I recognize that the Lord is my keeper and that he does not slumber or sleep, I can rest in his loving arms. I can have peace that surpasses all understanding. When you dedicate your life to Christ, it gives you courage to keep the faith and strength to stay in the race. Sometimes it is hard, but when we surrender to God we recognize that He is in control. Knowing that God is control gives us the perseverance to hold to His unchanging hand and let God do it.

In order to let God do it, you have to be still and know that God is God. You must stop relying on your own strength and ingenuity. The Word tells us, "That they who wait on the Lord shall renew their strength. They will mount up on wings like eagles. They will run and not grow weary; they will walk and not be faint" (Isaiah 40:1). Being still is a form of waiting. You are taking a moment to halt from all the busyness that is consuming your life and, for a moment, going to a quiet and tranquil place so you can hear from the Lord. You do not have to tell the Lord anything. "Your Father knows that you have need of these things before you ask" (Matthew 6:8). God has already prepared for us everything that we need. We just have to stop and ask for guidance.

A preacher opened up her sermon recently with the acronym H.A.L.T. It was based on a devotional by Charles Stanley she read that addressed the fact that the enemy, Satan, likes to attack us when we are weak and vulnerable—when we are hungry, angry, lonely, and tired. We often get to these places of vulnerability because we are operating in our own strength. We decide what we want and we try to do anything and everything to get what we want or what we think we need. But if we take time to listen to Lord, we will find that He has a plan for us. If we would just halt, we would recognize that they are plans to prosper us and not to harm us; plans to give us a hope and a future.

Once you recognize the plan that God has for your life, you will be more concerned about what God thinks than what people think. You can serve the Lord with gladness. In her devotional, *Love Out Loud,* Joyce Meyer focuses on Joshua and how he and his house chose to serve the Lord. In Jesus' time many believers would not confess their faith to others because they feared expulsion from the synagogue if they went public with their belief in Jesus. They cared too much about people's approval. It still happens today. But I challenge you to be like Joshua, who was bold in his belief in God, declaring that, "as for me and my house, we will serve the Lord" (Joshua 24:15). Be like Joshua, and determine that you and your household will serve the Lord. Make a deliberate, personal decision to serve the Lord and boldly declare, "As for me and my house, we will serve the Lord." Whether other people agree or not, serving and following God is the only way to live a fulfilling, victorious life. Jesus died to give you the freedom to follow the lead of the Holy Spirit. As you follow Him, I guarantee that He will lead you into a rewarding life.[1]

When you recognize Jesus Christ as your Lord and Savior and make a choice to be dedicated, faithful, loyal and committed to Christ, things in your life will begin to change. You will not only serve the Lord with gladness, but you will serve in God's strength. God gives us eternal hope by lifting us up, washing us clean, and setting our feet upon a new and solid path as described in Psalm 40:2. But what should we now do since our feet have been set? When we are in the slimy and muddy pit we are vulnerable to attack. It's difficult to move and we easily lose our balance. We tend to live in fear—not knowing who to trust or which way to turn. But as Christ lifts us up we become "a new creation" (2 Corinthians 5:17). "Life on solid ground should not be the same as life in the pit! That's worth

---

[1] Meyer, Joyce. Love Out Loud. FaithWords, 2011.

repeating - Life should NOT be the same!!"[1] That should give us motivation to move forward and do the things that God is calling us to do.

As the Spirit of God transforms us, He also provides everything we need to accomplish His work and live a victorious life, "His divine power has given us everything we need for life and godliness" (2 Peter 1:3). Knowing that our Heavenly Father has created us anew and gifted us with ALL we ever need, we must now be resolved to stand firm. "Therefore, my dear brothers, stand firm. Let nothing move you. Always give yourselves fully to the work of the Lord, because you know that your labor in the Lord is not in vain" (1 Corinthians 15:58). We must make every effort to firmly stand; and yet, we must realize we cannot stand in our own strength. The ground is solid only because of Christ. He IS the rock upon which we have been set—the Rock of our Salvation. Whenever we feel unworthy or unable to follow, whenever we feel we can no longer stand, we have surely begun to look to our own strength rather than God. "Now it is God who makes both us and you stand firm in Christ" (2 Corinthians 1:21). He alone gives us the strength.

We have trusted Him to lift us out of the pit; and now that we are His child; we must continue to trust Him to strengthen us and be the Rock of our life. "For if, when we were God's enemies, we were reconciled to Him

---

[1] Steve Troxel, God's Daily Word Ministries, March 17, 2014

through the death of His Son, how much more, having been reconciled, shall we be saved through His life!" (Romans 5:10). The solid Rock is no place to tremble, no place to fear. He will remain solid for all eternity; and, as we stand on Him, He will accomplish through us what we are unable to do in our own strength. He is our new life, our strength, our identity, and all our self-worth. He is our comfort when we grieve and He is our guiding light when we have lost our way. Let's honor our Heavenly Father as we continue to stand. Let's bring Him glory as we resolve to stand firm on the Rock!

My theme scripture for life has been my rock. This scripture summarizes how I walk in ministry: "I do not let this Book of the Law (the Word of God) depart from my mouth. I meditate on it day and night, so that I may be careful to do everything written in it. Then, I will be prosperous and successful" (Joshua 1:8). In order to walk this out, I have to say "yes" to the Lord. Shekinah Glory Ministries has a song called "Yes," and the song asks the question, "Will your heart and soul say yes?" God speaks to me through the song and asks, "If I told you what I really need from you, would your heart and soul say yes?" Then the song gently, but urgently, challenges the listener to say, "Yes!" The challenge is to not just simply say yes but to proclaim that I will obey Jesus. The challenge is to emphatically state that I will not stray from Jesus. The call is to declare that I have made up my mind to say "yes."

The song says, "My soul says yes! My mind says yes! My heart says yes!" Deliverance is available to you when you are willing to say yes and surrender all to Christ.

Saying yes helps you to maintain your sanity and stay focused on the plan that God has for you. There will be battles to fight, but God says, "I'll fight your battle—mind, body and soul." The battle is already won if you think on these things... "Whatever is true, whatever is noble, whatever is right, whatever is pure, whatever is lovely, whatever is admirable—if anything is excellent or praiseworthy—think about such things" (Philippians 4:8 NIV). Ephesians 4:23 in the Amplified Bible says, "And be constantly renewed in the spirit of your mind [having a fresh mental and spiritual attitude]." Whether you contributed to the situation in which you currently find yourself, or whether it is through no fault of your own, the potter does not want to leave you where you are. He wants to put you back together again, but you must trust and believe that she can. Every season is not going to be warm and sunny. We are going to experience fall and winter, but I am here to let you know that spring and summer are coming. Better is coming and you can move forward.

You move forward by saying "yes, Lord" to His will and to His way. Once you surrender the release from bondage comes, and you begin to develop your relationship with the Lord. When you have surrendered

your all—when you have made the decision to say yes—
you have made up your mind to do what the Lord says to
do and to say what the Lord tells you to say. You have
determined that if God will lead you, you will go. You have
made a conscious decision to submit your way to God's
way. There is more that God requires of all of us, and if we
are to be delivered and move forward in our freedom we
must say "yes." God is calling us higher, so hold on and let
God do it. There is so much more that God has for us to
do, and we cannot be afraid of men and women in our
faces. God is calling us out of our dry place. It is a process.
We must make a decision to be dedicated and committed
to Christ. I made a decision to follow Jesus, no turning
back, no turning—the world behind me, the cross before
me—no turning back. Once I made the decision to
dedicate my life to Christ, I became passionate about life. I
became focused on avid, active living.

AVID ACTIVE LIVING

In order to experience release from whatever is keeping you bound, you need to live an active life. You must also have something to focus on so that you can press forward and not be bogged down in your current condition as you journey towards deliverance. Remember, it is just a season. Be avid about an activity, a cause, a practice or a hobby. Merriam-webster.com provides two definitions of avid. The definition listed first can almost be perceived as negative—"desirous to the point of greed: urgently eager". When avid is used here, however, it is more applicable to the second definition—characterized by enthusiasm and vigorous pursuit". I am talking about a vigorous pursuit of passion. Passion: *a strong feeling of enthusiasm or excitement for something or about doing something.* Passion gives you purpose. When you are avid about a thing it gives you the drive to move forward. As I write this book, my desire to be a published author is pushing me forward. I am disciplined to accomplish my goal.

When the trials of life are weighing you down it may seem impossible to be passionate. However, in order to experience liberation from whatever has you mentally, physically, or spiritually bound you have to press through the pain by pursuing your passion. It is a process. You need to have an avid interest in something rather than wallowing in your hurt and pain. What brings you joy? Knitting hats for children at St. Jude? Painting? Reading? Volunteering at a church or homeless shelter? Running? If you are not experiencing any joy right now, think back to what you used to be excessively eager about doing and reflect on what you can do now, in the present, to rekindle that feeling. Many athletes have experienced physical hurts that have kept them from playing the game, but their love of sports inspired them to work with young athletes to help them pursue their dreams. Life's circumstances and situations are constantly changing, but that does not mean that you stop living. Put your passion to work in another place.

When you do something that you are passionate about it can bring you personal release or joy (i.e., running). You can also do something that, while it brings you joy, can also bring that same satisfaction to others. For example, you may love to knit, which brings you joy. So you knit hats for the children at St. Jude Children's Research Hospital in Memphis, Tennessee, which brings them joy. Whatever the case, you need to do something purposeful so that you are not bogged down in your situation.

Although I love to read and journal, dance is what helped bring me out my situation. I found release in the liturgical dance ministry. The fellowship of women was a blessing. The first year in the ministry I traveled a lot for work, so I missed a lot of practices. The first piece that I learned and kept in my heart was Kurt Carr's "For Every Mountain." During the time that we were learning and preparing to minister this piece, I was transitioning. As described earlier, my job situation had taken a drastic change for the worse. I was struggling to trust God. Shortly after ministering this piece in dance, which was an awesome spiritual experience, my world came crashing down around me. But, I kept giving God praise.

I kept giving God praise for every mountain that he brought me over. Because I made it over the mountains and through the valleys, my dream was still alive. Gospel artist William Murphy's song "Dream" says *It is never too late to be what you should have been. It is never too late to start over again. Dream!* Pursuing your passion can give you new life. It gives you the motivation to do what you should have done and recognize *the curses are gone, you are the chosen one.* One of the reasons people experience bondage is because they did not get to do what they always wanted to do. Maybe they did not accomplish what they wanted in their career. Maybe they did not attain something that they desired—own a new home, earn a degree, or get married and have children. But, it is never too late to chase after your dream. What God has prepared your eyes have never seen. *Today is the day that God is going to change your name. Dream!* Pursue your aspiration.

Many people are bitter because they wanted to achieve a certain goal or obtain a certain item, but for whatever reason they did not accomplish their objective or obtain their desired material possession when they were young. Many carry that bitterness further into their adult lives and played the blame- or the pity game. People will blame everybody under the sun, from their parents, siblings, and other family members to their classmates, bosses, and coworkers, as being responsible for keeping them from achieving their dreams and desires. Others will have a pity party where they want people to feel sorry for them because something happened (or did not happen) when they were young, so now they cannot achieve their dream.

Everyone has a past and it cannot be changed. But you do not have to stay in bondage to your past. Instead, allow it to enlarge your future. As was stated in chapter one, I focused on my education to elevate myself out of a life of physical and emotional poverty. As a result, I have done and seen things I never would have been exposed to if I limited myself to my rural hometown. I am not saying leave home and never look back. You leave home to experience a new environment, which provides an opportunity for expansion and growth that can be shared with those back home. Of course, I may have gone to the extreme in attempting to capture a new life, but I bounced back. Even though something happened in your far past—

you were born into a challenging life circumstance—or something happened in your recent past (like last week or yesterday), you do not have stay there. Use your past to propel yourself into your future.

Today is the first day of the rest of your life. The moment is now, so start now. For people's birthdays on Facebook I post, "Have a wonderful and blessed birthday! EnJOY today for the present that it is." Every day that you are in the present is a present, and God is calling you to pursue the promise by using your gifts. God has bestowed gifts to each and every one of us. What we are passionate about is where our gifts reside.

If you are not sure what your gifts are, there are several tools available to help you identify that which you are graced to do. There are spiritual gifts tests that identify your gifts in ministry. There are personality tests, such as Myers-Briggs, that help identify the vocation for which you are best suited and would most likely achieve success. Recognize that often what we do Monday through Friday at our nine-to-five jobs to pay the bills is not what gives us true joy. If you have a career that fully optimizes your gifts, fantastic. Carry that over into activities outside of work. But if your job is just that—a job—do not give up hope. You can still find your place of enjoyment through a hobby or activity outside of work. Pursue your passion with a purpose.

When you have a purpose you are intentional. When you are going through it may be difficult to keep the momentum to pursue your purpose. It will be difficult to stay motivated to keep moving toward your goal, but you have to stay in the race. If you cannot do a full run, slow down to a jog. If the jogging gets too intense, pace a walk, but keep moving until you can get back to a run. If you stay in the race, the finish line will come. Once you see the finish line it will motivate you to break into a sprint. Once that race is complete you will look back and be able to say, "I made it!" Not only that, you will have strength for the next marathon, because if you did it before you can do it again with the power of God operating within you.

As I wrote this book, I participated in a coaching course. We motivated each other through conference calls and a team website. One month we took a challenge to write at least three hundred words per day. We encouraged each other on the team site and held each other accountable. You cannot do it alone. Find a champion. Find someone who can cheer you on. Keep moving toward your goal. The promise is in view.

My motivation came through my liturgical dance ministry. There were many days when I just did not want to move from the couch or get out of the bed, but I pressed my way. Philippians 3:14 NIV says, "I press toward the mark for the prize of the high calling of God in Christ Jesus." And press I did. Our theme scripture is Romans

12:1 KJV, which says, "I beseech you therefore, brethren, by the mercies of God, that ye present your bodies a living sacrifice, holy, acceptable unto God, which is your reasonable service." Although it was a struggle, I committed to present my body as a living sacrifice and worship the Lord through the dance. I made a commitment to worship the Lord in spirit and in truth with each movement of my body. Since I was part of a ministry, I could not just sit it out. There were people checking on me and looking for me. There were people holding me accountable so that I would not die but live and proclaim what the Lord has done. Despite what had happened in my life, my life was not over. The race is not given to the swift or the strong, but to the one who endures until the end. God is calling us all to run the race marked out for us with perseverance (Hebrews 12:1).

During one Women's Season at church, we ministered a piece based on Kurt Carr's "Just the Beginning." The lyrics start out, *It's just the beginning, there is so much God has in store. Just the beginning, it is not the end, it is just the overture.* An overture or a prelude is an introduction to an event that one anticipates will have a grand finale. But you have to keep moving; you have to stay in the race to achieve the grand finale. The song further goes on to say, *I know you are blessed but you still haven't seen God's best. I already know God's been good to you. I already know God's been faithful to you. I already know...He has done some incredible things. But I declare and I decree; I prophesy with authority: You haven't seen your best days yet. You haven't seen your greatest victory yet. This is just the beginning.* Then he asks, *do you receive the prophecy?* The song stands on 1 Corinthians 2:9 as the Kurt Carr Singer's belt out, *eyes haven't seen the things God sees in you. Ears haven't heard the plans he is planning just for you. Neither has it entered into the hearts of man all of the good things that my God has in store.* They continue on with *there is so much more. I already know—God has been good to you. God has been faithful to you. He has done some incredible things but I declare and I decree, I prophesy with authority...you haven't seen your best days yet. You haven't seen your greatest victory yet. This is just the beginning.*

At the end of song when Kurt Carr began to prophesy, we as ministers of the dance took the position of athletes—as runners. We were ready for "on the mark, get set, go." And when he said, *I prophetically proclaim. Hold on to your dreams. Be steadfast to your vision. It shall come to pass,* we were off! We held on as he proclaimed, *gifted athlete, don't quit! Victory is right around the corner,* and we said in our minds along with the soloist, *I'm just getting started...it is not over!* Philippians 1:6 says, "He who hath begun a good work in you shall perform it," so you just have to *hold on, hold on, hold on...this is just the beginning.* Kurt Carr posed the question again; *do you receive the prophecy?* He spoke the vision and made it plain; *talented musician. Gifted musician. Don't despise your small beginnings. Preacher keep preaching. Teacher, keep teaching. Student, don't get weary. There is an incredible future ahead of you. This is just the beginning.* That song ministered to me then and it ministers to me now. Don't give up; this is just the beginning. No matter how old or young you are, pursue your passion. It is never too late to go back to school. It is never too late to write a book. It is never too late to help someone along the way. Work the work that God is calling you to work while it is day, because night time is coming when no person can work. Avidly live the active life that God is calling you to live. It is your inheritance.

The Word says, "For I know the plans I have for you. Plans to prosper you and not harm you. Plans to give you a hope and a future" (Jeremiah 29:11). If God has a plan for you—if God has a calling on your life—there is no timeline for fulfilling that plan except God's timeline. No matter how old you are, as long as you have breath in your body you can pursue the plan that God has for you. You can pursue your passion. Get avid with action. Take pleasure in your activities. Follow your dream—write the book, pursue the career path, start your business. Call to God and God will answer (Jeremiah 33:3). God promises a guarantee for greater. Your Creator will give you the desires of your heart. Pursue your passion and God will bring you out into your wealthy place. Deliverance is available to you through avid active living.

NOURISHED BY SPIRITUAL DISCIPLINES

A discipline is a practice or method of teaching, or enforcing acceptable patterns of behavior. When we refer to spiritual disciplines, we are referring to daily practices that increase our spiritual growth—habits that enhance our relationship with the Father. The number one spiritual practice for me is studying God's Word. The Word is our foundation. Each day when I arise I read several devotions. At least one of them leads me to a passage of scripture that I read in more depth. As a seminary student, one of the required first-year courses is Formation for Ministry, which focuses on spiritual disciplines. Each week we have an assignment sheet with three to five items, and inevitably we are to read some passage of scripture. Not just read it, but meditate on it.

There is a difference between meditating on the Bible and reading the Bible. Often, when you just read the Bible you will get to the end of a chapter and realize you understand little of what you just read. When you meditate on God's Word you think seriously about what you are reading. You are saying, "God, speak to me. Teach me. As I ponder Your Word, reveal its depth to me." We are to reflect on how the Word speaks to us. We are to let it guide our prayer. We are to raise questions to God and Jesus Christ. We are to read and be read by the text. The text is to challenge our call to ministry. We must make a habit of reading and studying God's Word every day so that it becomes a life practice. Aside from studying and experiencing the scriptures and other holy readings, there are other disciplines or practices that support our inward and outward journey.

Prayer is a vital spiritual practice. It can be silent and contemplative or it can be intercessory. Prayer is right up there with studying the Word. The two often go hand in hand because we are to pray the scriptures. When we make our requests to God or if we want to be sure we are praying God's will, then we need to pray God's Word; we need to pray Jesus' truth back to him. God's Word will not return back to him void. There is no certain way to pray. There is no certain time or posture. I often find myself on my knees by my bed when I arise early in the morning or sometimes before I go to bed at night.

The Word says to pray without ceasing and more often than not, I find myself communing with God as I get ready in the morning. I talk to God as I sit at my computer reading my devotionals. I talk to God in the bathroom as I shower and get ready for work. My favorite time is when I am commuting to work. Often a song on the radio or CD will bring me to a place of remembrance of what the Lord has done or a place of expectation of what the Lord is getting ready to do in my life. At that moment I just have to praise and thank Him. I don't ask for anything; I just thank God for being Jehovah in my life—Jireh (my provider), El Shaddai (the all sufficient one), my everything, my all and all.

Often I am led to intercede for others because my spirit grieves for them. I intercede for individuals and situations. As I intercede for others, and even situations in my own life, I am frequently led to fast and pray. Being intentional about fasting is a difficult practice for me because I love to eat. But time and again when the Lord is pressing me to fast, God takes away my appetite. I have no desire to eat because my mind is focused on the call to pray, whether for someone else or a situation in my own life.

If you feel you don't know how to pray, realize that prayer is simply about relationship. If you know how to carry on a conversation with another human being, you can pray and carry on a conversation with God. Prayer is two-way communication. It is not just about you talking to God. It is also about you having an open heart and open ears to hear what God is saying and more importantly to being obedient about what God is calling you to do. Prayers do not have to be formal, but if you want to expand your prayer life, there are several books that might give you insight into prayer.

Susan Gaddy Pope's Dancing My Prayers is an excellent resource. This book is for anyone, not just those called to dance. She states that "a dance between two people is an intimate conversation of what is in their hearts. God is asking each of us to dance with Him, delight in Him, worship Him and allow Him to move us." The book opens with Psalm 88:13, "But I, O Lord, cry out to you; in the morning, my prayer comes before you." The seven position dance prayer described in the book represents movement that brings one into the presence of the Lord every morning so you can hear God's voice throughout the day. Dancing your prayers allows you to really get the Word of God into your body (pg. 20). As you move in prayer, it can lead you to the next spiritual practice of honoring our bodies.

We are called to take care of ourselves physically. We cannot do the work that God is calling us to do if we are not physically fit. "Do you not know that your body is a temple of the Holy Spirit, who is in you, whom you have received from God? You are not your own: you were bought at a price. Therefore honor God with your body" (1Cor. 6:19-20). We prepare ourselves physically through healthful eating, drinking plenty of water, engaging in physical exercise, and resting. As with everything that we do as Christians, we must do unto God, including eating. 1 Corinthians 10:31 states, "So whether you eat or drink or whatever you do, do it all for the glory of God." Eating healthful meals not only means limiting fried foods, junk foods, etc., but it also means giving your body the proper nutrients so that it can be naturally fueled for the demands of your lifestyle.

It is also important that we keep our bodies hydrated. We should not only drink water during and after engaging in physical activity, but also throughout the day. According to WebMd.com, water helps energize muscles. The American College of Sports Medicine recommends people drink about 17 ounces of water or sports drink about two hours before exercise. We need to incorporate a balance of cardiovascular exercises, strength building exercises, and stretching.

It is also important that we rest. Not only do we need the recommended seven to eight hours of sleep each night, but we also need to take time to rest our minds and spirits. Remember that God only worked six days and rested on the seventh (Genesis 2:3). He instructs us to do the same. God knows that we must rest to recuperate, even in ministry. Mark 6:31 talks about how Jesus advised the disciples to rest from ministry saying, "And He said to them, 'Come away by yourselves to a secluded place and rest a while' (For there were many people coming and going, and they did not even have time to eat)." Resting goes in line with keeping the Sabbath. Jesus' voice in Mark 6:31 is his Sabbath voice—humble and gentle of heart, making no demands. Sabbath is the uncluttered time and space in which we can distance ourselves from our own activities enough to see what God is doing.

In order to experience a true Sabbath, you have to escape your normal routine. This is often difficult to do, even if you are able to get away from your physical location (i.e. work). I find that even when I take a day off specifically for a Sabbath rest, it is very difficult to just be still and know that God is God. If I stay home, I find myself doing "stuff" that needs to be done.

I attended a seminar recently where attendees were instructed to do only what was sustainable for us. The facilitator stated that balance was not about getting everything done but rather doing what was sustainable for us. We were charged to decide, delegate, and delete. She emphasized that we were not to delegate to our alter ego or to our day off. We were to delegate it to someone else and entrust them to get it done and not take it back later because we did not like the way they got it done. I am guilty of delegating to my day off. But that is not a genuine Sabbath. In order to experience the optimal peace and rest that a Sabbath is supposed to bring, one must be intentional.

The best Sabbath I ever experienced was when I went on vacation to Hawaii. Talk about casting your cares on the Lord and retreating from your normal routine for a little while. It was a group trip with a few tourist items on the agenda but for the most part you did what you wanted to do. I got up early many days because I am a morning person, and sat on the balcony of my room and watched the sunrise or watched (and listened) the waves in the ocean. I wrote in my journal, read my devotional and prayed. I experienced inner peace being away from it all just for a little awhile. This vacation allowed me the opportunity to re-energize and rejuvenate for the reality of life back home. Refresh. Renew. Restore. I recognize that we cannot all get away to Hawaii or a similar vacation spot on a regular basis.

We may not have the time or the finances, but "if we are not able to rest one day a week we are taking ourselves far too seriously (Peterson, "The Pastor's Sabbath," Leadership, Spring, 1985, pp. 55-56). God is calling us to draw away and spend some time with our Creator. In God we live, and move, and have our very being. We are God's offspring. We must make the sacrifice to separate ourselves and hear a Word from the Lord so we can better serve God's people.

As you decide what you can sustainably do (i.e. while maintaining good health, getting six to eight hours of sleep each night, etc.) and what you can delegate to other people, the rest must be deleted from your list as unimportant. If the activities are not life-giving, then let them go. Surrender to God! Draw away for a day or weekend or go to a bed and breakfast. I experience a morning Sabbath right in the comfort of my own bedroom listening to Marvin Sapp's Thirsty CD. "Place of Worship" and "In the Garden" speak to me. The Sabbath is about finding your place of worship.

I've come to the garden alone while the dew is still on the roses and the voice I hear falling on my ear, the sound of God discloses. He speaks in the sound of his voice. It's so sweet that the birds they hush their singing and the melody that he sings to me within my heart is still ringing. And God walks with me, and God talks with me and He tells me that I am his own. And the joy we share as we tarry we there...none other has ever been known. Do not miss the opportunity of Sabbath rest. As you sacrifice and separate in preparation for serving the Lord better, you will find benefits to your spirit, soul, and body outweigh the sacrifice. You cannot give God your best when you are not your best. In order to be your best you must steal away for a little while to renew.

When you are renewed, you are able to focus on other disciplines. God is calling us to be good stewards of our resources, both financial and environmental. There are many tools available to provide guidance on financial stewardship. I receive a monthly newsletter called *Game Time Budgeting,* which is authored by a Christian couple. It contains practical financial information based on the Word of God. The earth is the Lord's and the fullness thereof, and the Lord wants us to take care of the Earth. God wants his people to maintain an ecological balance. Recycle. Walk instead of drive. The Lord desires that we use everything that he has provided to us to bring him glory and honor as we go through this journey called life.

Committing to spiritual practices and making them habits will prepare us in our daily lives.

In a *From Faith to Faith* daily devotional Kenneth Copeland says: When you're up against the wall, don't start begging God to break through it for you. That's not the way He works. He'll give you the plan. He'll give you the power. And He'll guarantee the victory. But your hand, not His own, is the instrument He's going to use to get the job done. You're going to have to stretch forth your hand by speaking and acting on the Word, even when circumstances are against you. Don't wait for God to slay the dragon in your life. You have the sword of the Spirit, the all-powerful Word of the living God, at your fingertips. Pick it up and use it today!

God has given us tools and expects us to use them. Just as food will not provide any physical nourishment unless it is eaten, the Word, prayer, and other spiritual disciplines will not provide nourishment unless they are practiced. O taste and see that the Lord is good! (Psalm 34:8).

CARE FOR THE SOUL

Care for the soul is essential for deliverance. One cannot overcome unless the soul is whole. In *The Message* translation, 1 Thessalonians 5:23 says, "May God Himself make you holy and whole – spirit, soul, and body." The soul relates to the mind. The human mind is the center of our thought and behavior. If our thoughts and behavior are not in balance, then our emotional and mental health are not in balance. As you experience the various trials and tribulations in your life, praying and going to church may not be enough. God is always there but God works through humans. Find a person in whom you can trust—a confidant. You may need to seek professional counseling. In the workplace you can find help through employee assistance programs. Many churches offer professional counseling.

My church has a "Center for the Soul," which is available to address the emotional and mental health needs of our congregation and those in the community. The Center provides a wide range of services for those whose life journeys have presented a challenge in coping and moving forward. The goal is to offer compassionate, Christ-centered counsel, guidance, and external referrals where appropriate. Individual and group sessions deal with grief, divorce, abuse, rape, family distress, and conflict resolution. All of these are issues which can cause emotional and physical bondage if not addressed in a timely manner. Spiritual disciplines are essential but sometimes professional help is necessary. The key is getting to the root of the matter. What is the underlying issue for what you are dealing with? What is the underlying issue for your behavior?

Sometimes it is easy to get to the problem. When an otherwise well–behaved child starts acting out, for example, and you start to question why, you may soon find that the parents recently divorced or that the child recently lost a parent. Because the child does not know how to deal with the loss, she acts out to ease the pain or fill a void in her life. Or when a once active and jubilant adult begins acting despondent, you may immediately realize that this change is due to loss of a spouse or a child. Another scenario is you may learn that she is having a hard struggle with the empty nest syndrome. When you can easily identify the underlying issue, you can help the person get help.

Everyone has issues and has to deal with them in his or her own way, but it is good to have a circle of friends that will walk with a person at their own pace. Sometimes those friends may have to show you some tough love if you are walking a bit too slowly. While we all have issues, we have to continue to live life as we deal with our difficulties. Setbacks should not be permanent obstacles that keep us from fulfilling God's purpose for our lives.

You may have lost a loved one or lost a job, but you have to keep living. Just as birthday parties and wedding receptions do not last forever, pity parties must come to an end. Allow others to help you come out of the darkness into the marvelous light.

Of course, it is not always easy to identify the root of the matter. When everything seems okay on the outside and you really do not realize that your past is dramatically impacting your present and your future, it is hard to get help. You are not going to seek help if you are not aware that you need help. Your circle of friends is not going to intercede on your behalf if they do not realize that there is problem. My past was not uncommon. You hear many people talk about how they grew up poor. When many celebrities are interviewed, they discuss how they grew up in single-parent households with limited resources. You hear stories of families with lots of siblings growing up in a one or two bedroom house or apartment. There are rural poor and urban poor, but at the end of the day, poor is poor.

When people give their testimonies as adults, they are sharing how they made it over. Despite their small beginnings, through education, hard work, and diligence they have made good lives for themselves. Many are now able to help take care of their families and go back to help build up the communities where they grew up; it is about making a difference. But somewhere between the humble beginnings and the testimony there is the test. I did not recognize the root of my test until many later years, and it stemmed from humble beginnings which led me to satisfy my flesh instead of pursuing the things of God. I was seeking acceptance from people and trying to gratify myself with "stuff".

In the midst of convincing myself that my stuff was going to make me happy and that another human being was going to make me whole, I was missing the fact that the only One who could bring joy and make me whole was Jesus Christ. As I stood on the precipice of a breakdown due to financial stress, there was a major war going on between my Spirit and my flesh. As I was seeking to draw closer to God, the enemy was trying to keep me drawn into the world. Yes, we have to live in this world, but if you are a child of the most high King, you are not *of* the world. I was baptized at an early age and accepted Jesus Christ as my Lord and Savior. Once you belong to the Father, you may be oppressed by strongholds, but you cannot be possessed by the enemy. And, Jesus is able to break the strongholds. There is power in the name of Jesus to break every chain.

A young preacher at a youth revival reminded the congregation that Jesus had to carry his cross and walk with his pressure. Jesus had to walk with it so that he could help us walk with it. However, I was trying to walk it alone and not let anyone know what I was going through financially. Even as I made feeble attempts to deal with my credit, I still did not give full disclosure because I was just embarrassed and in disbelief of where I stood. I sought the advice of Christian financial counselors and read Dave Ramsey's book, but I still did not follow through on the advice. Until things broke, I was convinced that as long as I was working and able to pay my bills everything would be okay. But one day it was not okay, and once I fell off the cliff I had to get help.

Of course I got immediate help during my stay in the hospital, but that was just to deal with the issue at hand. I had a chemical imbalance in my brain. I experienced a manic episode which is defined as "a period of predominant mood elevation, expansiveness, or irritation together with some combination of inflated self-esteem or grandiosity, decreased need of sleep, talkativeness, flight of ideas, distractibility, hyperactivity, hypersexuality, and recklessness".[1] Another way to define recklessness is "involvement in activities with potentially dire consequences, e.g. buying sprees, sexual indiscretions, and inappropriate business transactions"[2]. Reckless spending and buying sprees were my demise.

Losing my job and not being able to maintain the financial fiasco that I had created was the trigger that set

---

[1] http://medical-dictionary.thefreedictionary.com/manic+episode

[2] http://medical-dictionary.thefreedictionary.com/manic+episode

everything off. If I had paid attention to the signs or listened to others close to me when they made comments about my behavior, maybe I could have gotten help sooner. But sometimes you have to hit rock bottom before you get help. And believe it or not, getting hospitalized and diagnosed was not my rock bottom. I was in denial for a long time and ended up getting hospitalized again.

Once I accepted that my diagnosis was real, the real pity party began. I went through a major bout of depression and it was almost another four years after my second hospitalization that I was delivered and set free. A part of my journey to deliverance was meeting with counselors. I had counseling sessions with members of the ministerial staff at my church, and I also sought the help of professional counselors. It was not necessarily a choice I made on my own, especially in the beginning. There were friends around me who knew what was going on and they continued to press and stay engaged in my life. They did not allow me to drift away even though I may have wanted to do so.

One year my friends even contacted my mother to come check on me under the auspices of coming to our annual Women's Retreat. A mother knows and it was after her visit that I really began to have some breakthroughs. It was a continuous struggle but I had to keep pressing. Just like Jesus had to walk with his pressure, I had to walk with mine. Despite what I was going through, despite my circumstances, I still had to live day to day. That is all that God is calling us to do—live one day at time. He said to give no worry about tomorrow, for tomorrow will worry about itself. Each day has enough trouble of its own (Matthew 6:24).

I listened to the counselors and eventually did the things required to get myself better and improve my quality of life. I wrote in a journal to cope and express my feelings, which allowed me to stand up for my feelings. We have to work with and through our feelings in order to maintain a healthy outlook and attitude. Denial used to be my default for handling intense emotions. If someone hurt me, rather than face the pain and confront them, I would shut down. I had to learn to speak out, especially where it came to medicine.

There were instances where I had to use discernment and realize that some professionals did not have my best interest in mind, particularly where it came to medicine management. There are some doctors who will attempt to keep you on high dosages of medicine for an undefined period of time. It is okay to ask questions, and if you are experiencing side effects it is okay to ask for changes. If the changes are not working, it is okay to get a second opinion or seek treatment from another healthcare professional. The key is to get help.

Professional counseling may be necessary to maintain a healthful lifestyle and there is no shame in seeking counseling. It does not mean you are crazy. There is nothing wrong with having to take medication if necessary. You do not have to share everything with everybody, but you have to share with somebody. God is a keeper if you want to be kept. You have an assignment, and if you walk in the Spirit, God will help you fulfill it. As a minister the first rule of pastoral care is self-care. You have to be healthy to help others.

Do not let others penetrate your boundaries. The word "no" is a complete sentence. Manage your boundaries by deciding to do what is sustainable for you, delegating other important things and deleting the rest. Knowing when and how to draw lines in our relationships helps us avoid unnecessary stress and keeps us from becoming overwhelmed. "No" creates the boundaries that are critical to helping us establish and maintain our identities.

The ultimate Counselor is the Holy Spirit. In John 14:26 KJV, Jesus tells us that "the Counselor, the Holy Spirit, whom the Father will send in my name, will teach you all things and will remind you of everything I have said to you." Jesus goes on further in verse 27 to say, "Peace I leave with you; my peace I give you. I do not give to you as the world gives. Do not let your hearts be troubled and do not be afraid". With God on your side, there is no reason to fear. You can have peace in the midst of the storm as you press towards your deliverance. God has not left us comfortless. Sometimes we have to be still and know that God is God and listen to what he has to say in our spirit. There are other times when God speaks to us through other human beings.

If we are in tune with the Father and have our ears of discernment open we will realize that God is speaking to us. It may be a friend or a family member. It could be a co-worker or classmate. Even as we seek professional help, God can speak to us through the counselors. God can and will use anyone or anything to His glory. If you trust and believe that deliverance is available to you, just reach out and touch the hem of his garment and you will be made whole.

EVIDENTLY TRANSPARENT

Evidently transparent is a tautology for sure, but one that I find necessary. Evidently is used to say that something is obvious. Transparent means something (or someone) is easily detected or seen through. It means that they are readily understood...obvious. When I speak of evidently transparent I am talking about authenticity. I have come to realize that I truly value authenticity and honesty. I see so many hurt people always playing make believe or trying to be carbon copies of someone else. In order to be evidently transparent you must be authentic. The bottom line is that you must be *you*.

God made each of us with a unique eternal design. The creative process is the progressive, orderly arrangement of things until what is seen outwardly lines up with what has already been seen inwardly. God is the Ultimate Creator. We find that He established an order of things before He ever brought them into being—an eternal purpose that He purposed in Christ. The crucifixion of Christ was not God's startled reaction to the unforeseen and unimaginable fall of Adam. God envisioned things straight through to the end before He set them in motion. If you want to move forward to do things that God is calling you to do, you must begin the creative process of outwardly transforming what has already been seen inwardly. Live the truth that God is calling you to live.

Where the Spirit of the Lord is, there is freedom (2 Corinthians 3:17).

I read a book recently that said colleges these days are breeding grounds for poor decisions, emotional brokenness, and sharp pain. I would like to add to that by saying that life in general is a breeding ground for poor decisions, emotional brokenness, and sharp pain! Just as this is an internal struggle for the college student (because the girl who was raped during her freshman year and the guy who hates himself and struggles with depression do not seem broken when sitting in class), it is also an internal struggle for most people. Many adults give the appearance that all is well with the world; they only want people to see the good. But a preacher once said "life is a mixture of joys and pains," and to get through this thing we call life, we have to be transparent...*evidently transparent.*

I am not saying that you should tell everything to everybody. And, I am also not saying that you should always be transparent by sharing your "woe is me" story with everyone that you come across in a despondent "nobody knows the troubles I've seen" manner. That is not effective because most people do not care—not because they are mean and uncaring, but because they have problems of their own. Share the words of your testimony to bring healing and deliverance to someone else. Let the Holy Spirit direct you on when, where, and to whom you are evidently transparent because your transparency can help someone along the way. People do not flaunt their brokenness when trying to prove themselves. But in their dorm rooms (and bedrooms) in the middle of the night after another disaster, they become transparent over and over again.

As people are currently going through - when they think they cannot make it another day - they sometimes share this with people whom they believe truly care about them. If you are the person with whom they choose to share, that is the time for you to be transparent about YOUR journey. The story they tell is their trial (right now)—the story you tell is your testimony. In describing a "test-im-on-y" a preacher once said the ANSWER to the QUESTION "Y" to the "TEST" "IM" "ON" may not come until the end. Once you have made it through to the end, share your story because it just may help someone along the way. It is the strength of our witness that leads others to Christ.

I was not always transparent. I never shared how I grew up because I was embarrassed. When my mother grew up poor in a house without indoor plumbing, it was okay because that is how a lot of people, especially blacks, grew up back then. In the "old days" that was acceptable living. However, when I grew up in the eighties it was not acceptable and as a teenager struggling to fit in and be liked, it was just not cool. I did not do a lot of things as a teenager, not because my mother kept me from doing them but because I believed in reciprocity. I probably did not even know what that word meant at the time, but I was very conscious of what I did and what I allowed myself to be exposed to because I knew that I could not, or should I say would not, reciprocate.

I did not accept invitations to sleepovers, birthday parties or various other events that would call for me to reciprocally invite people to my home. If I slept over at someone's house, they would be looking to sleepover at mine. If I went to a birthday party at someone's house, they would be looking to come to my birthday party. I never even had a birthday party as a child or a teenager. There was no sweet sixteen party for me, but then I wasn't asking for one. Where was it going to be held? Who was going to pay for it?

I held tight to myself to prevent from getting hurt. I had a lot of acquaintances but very few that I called friends. Everyone knew me at school. I was liked but I was not "popular". Since I could not be popular I chose to be smart. Education and knowledge were my weapons of warfare to get out.

I really have nothing extremely memorable, neither positive nor negative, from my high school years. I just went from year to year doing well academically and participating in the extracurricular activities I needed to put on my college applications. But, my life at home was totally different. Once I was home I was isolated from the world and I loved it.

Growing up we lived next door to my maternal grandmother and one thing my brother and I always got on our birthday was a cake. My brother's birthday is in the summer so we were out of school. I can remember it like it was yesterday—being in my Moy's kitchen watching her bake that cake. Sometimes it was chocolate on chocolate. Sometimes it was chocolate on yellow. It was always moist. It was always delicious. It was during those times that I did not care where I lived, what I wore, or what the world thought of me.

I loved my grandmother and I wish that she were still here today. She was the first grandparent that I lost. She left too early as a result of an untimely diagnosis of breast cancer. She came from a generation that did not believe in going to the doctor. She rubbed liniment on everything and by the time the cancer was discovered, it was too late. It had spread throughout her body and there was not much that the doctors could do but try to keep her comfortable. I loved my Moy and I miss her.

My sixteenth year was bitter sweet because she was gone and I did not get my chocolate cake that year. But as I sit back and reflect, it lets me know that the simple things in life are the important things. It is not about impressing people and trying to be something that you are not; it is about knowing who you are and accepting yourself for who you are. That does not mean that you should not strive to get better. It means that as you strive to get better, maintain your core. Your character is what makes you. It is not the neighborhood that you live in, the car that you drive, or the purse that you carry. It is your moral fiber. It is your make-up. It is the person that is individually you. God only made one of you. Psalm 139:13-14 in NRSV says, "For it was you who formed my inward parts; you knit me together in my mother's womb. I praise you, for I am fearfully and wonderfully made. Wonderful are your works; that I know very well." I am fearfully and wonderfully made. If that is so, why was I trying to become something I thought I was supposed to be based on the standards of the world?

God's standard is the standard. God said in Isaiah 55:8-9, "my thoughts are not your thoughts, neither are your ways my ways. For as the heavens are higher than the earth, so are My ways higher than your ways and My thoughts than your thoughts". If that is the case then we might as well just put ourselves in the hands of almighty God and rest in the knowledge that He is good and knows what's best. And all things do work together for good...all things are not good, but they surely do work together for good for those who love the Lord and are the called according to his purpose.

I know this now but did not back then. Once I finished college and left home I was focused on becoming the new Joy. When I started working, my entire check went toward paying bills, so I had little cash on which to live, which resulted in a vicious cycle of living on credit. Instead of trying to get my spending under control and pay off some debt, I returned to graduate school. Although I had a grant which covered one hundred percent of my tuition, I still had to obtain student loans to live on. Also, I worked on campus in the business school library administrative office because I refused to live like a college student. No one would have known because I looked like I had it all together. Even when I heard other people share their financial situations and circumstances, I would keep my mouth closed. I wanted to keep up appearances.

But now I am not caught up in keeping up with the Joneses or anyone else. I am learning every day the importance of enjoying life and living in the moment. Not recklessly but appreciatively, as I reflect on who God is and what God has done in my life. Allen Saunders said that life is what happens when we are busy making plans. Life indeed changes at every moment. Living this thing called life is a mixture of joy and pain. We as believers say that God is in control. We say that God is omnipresent, omnipotent, and omniscient. We say God is a Comforter, a Shield, a Help, a Lily in the Valley. We sing of his greatness. We sing that every praise is to our God. But we cannot just say these things. We have to believe them and live like we believe them. God is truly a keeper if you want to be kept.

When I first began the process of writing this book, in the midst being evidently transparent, one of the things I was concerned about was how my mother would respond. I know my mother, and I did not want her to read the book, particularly the first couple of chapters, and feel like what happened in my life was her fault—that if I had not grown up the way that I did, that I would not have ended up in the hospital. On my forty-fifth birthday I shared the first chapter of my book with a group of people that I considered my supporters for various reasons. One of them was my mother. It took her a while before she read the chapter—or at least a while before she responded. Eventually I got an e-mail with the subject "read" and it said, "I have read your pages from your book. I hope you know that I did the very best I could. I am also very proud of the accomplishments that you all have made. I truly enjoyed the times that I had with you all when you were growing up!"

Live through it...James Fortune and Fiya have a song called "Live Through It". And the fact of the matter is that no matter how wonderful or not so wonderful you grow up. No matter if you grow up with a platinum spoon in your mouth or a plastic one, life is going to happen and you just have to "live through it". It is not about what happened yesterday but how you respond to it. Are you going to keep living in yesterday and complaining about coulda, shoulda, woulda? Are you going to blame your mother, father, sister, brother for what they did that kept you from doing what you wanted to do yesterday or are you going to recognize today for the present that it is and use it to press forward to a better tomorrow?

No, tomorrow is not promised. But as long as we have light today, God is calling us to work. It is not just for today but in preparation for tomorrow, for when night time comes no man or woman can work. What are you postponing? Stop putting on a front. Be transparent about your situation and get some help so you can move forward and do what God is calling you to do. Deliverance is available to you and with the Holy Spirit as your motivation you can move forward. Keep pressing forward to touch the hem of his garment and you will be made whole. Keep pressing. Keep trusting. Keep believing. Deliverance is available to you.

ABOUT THE AUTHOR

Rev. Joy L. Wilkerson, native of Roxboro, NC, has been a Memphis resident since 1998. She is an Itinerant Deacon in the African Methodist Episcopal (AME) Church, and is an associate minister at Saint Andrew AME Church. Rev. Joy lives by Philippians 4:6 and truly believes in presenting everything to God with praise and thanksgiving.

Rev. Joy has been spreading the gospel via *The Word* e-mail devotional for over ten years. She is passionate about motivating others to move forward and walk worthy of the calling God has for their lives. The Lord called Joy to *write the vision and make it plain* sharing her testimony so others can be delivered and set free.

Rev. Joy earned a B.S. in Accounting, summa cum laude, from N.C. A & T State University and an MBA from The University of Michigan. As her relationship with the Lord increased, she was led to seminary. She graduated summa cum laude with a Master of Arts in Religion (MAR) from Memphis Theological Seminary (MTS) in May 2009 and is currently working on her Masters of Divinity.

Rev. Joy has been published in The A.M.E. Church Review. She is employed as a Program Design Analyst with a major third party administrator (TPA). She is a proud member of Delta Sigma Theta Sorority, Incorporated. She is the owner of one toy poodle named Jenks.